Genetics

by Lynn Van Gorp

Science Contributor
Sally Ride Science
Science Consultants
Thomas R. Ciccone, Science Educator
Ronald Edwards, Science Educator

MISSION:

Developed with contributions from Sally Ride Science™

Sally Ride
Science

Sally Ride Science™ is an innovative content company dedicated to fueling young people's interests in science.

Our publications and programs provide opportunities for students and teachers to explore the captivating world of science—from astrobiology to zoology.

We bring science to life and show young people that science is creative, collaborative, fascinating, and fun.

To learn more, visit www.SallyRideScience.com

First hardcover edition published in 2009 by
Compass Point Books
151 Good Counsel Drive
P.O. Box 669
Mankato, MN 56002-0669

Editor: Brenda Haugen
Designer: Heidi Thompson
Editorial Contributor: Sue Vander Hook

Art Director: LuAnn Ascheman-Adams
Creative Director: Keith Griffin
Editorial Director: Nick Healy
Managing Editor: Catherine Neitge

 This book was manufactured with paper containing at least 10 percent post-consumer waste.

Library of Congress Cataloging-in-Publication Data
Van Gorp, Lynn.
Genetics / by Lynn Van Gorp.
    p. cm. — (Mission: Science)
 Includes index.
ISBN 978-0-7565-3956-6 (library binding)
1. Genetics—Juvenile literature. I. Title. II. Series.
 QH437.5.V36 2009
 576.5—dc22   2008007720

Visit Compass Point Books on the Internet at *www.compasspointbooks.com*
or e-mail your request to *custserv@compasspointbooks.com*

Table of Contents

Genetics: The Basics

Have you ever thought about what your parents gave you when you were born? They may have given you a place to live, clothes to wear, and food to eat. But they gave you much more. They gave you their genes. Your father gave you half of your genes, and your mother gave you the other half.

Genes are the basic units of heredity. A zebra's genes give it stripes. A bird's genes give it wings. Our genes give us fingers and everything else that makes us human. Genes decide if our hair will be curly or straight, dark or light. They determine the size of our noses and the shape of our ears. The entire gene plan is called the genome, and it is found in our cells.

Each cell follows the instructions of the genes, which tell cells how to develop and what to do. And all the cells work together to make stripes, wings, or fingers.

A foal inherits half of its genes from its mother and half from its father.

Young meerkats, called pups, have characteristics of both their mother and father.

Gregor Mendel (1822—1844)

Gregor Johann Mendel is called the father of modern genetics. He was a monk who lived in Europe in what is now the Czech Republic. Mendel studied many kinds of peas, how they grew, and what made them unique. His curiosity about plants taught him a great deal about genes and heredity. Few people were aware of Mendel's work while he was alive. Today he may be the best-known scientist in the field of genetics.

Genes are passed along through reproduction. Each species reproduces its own kind—people make people, horses make horses, and trees make trees. Reproduction is necessary for a species to survive.

Asexual Reproduction

One form of reproduction is called asexual reproduction. That means something can reproduce all by itself, without a partner. A single cell simply divides and forms two new cells. The new cells are identical to the parent cell.

Within the nucleus of each cell are chromosomes, threadlike structures that carry genes. Human body cells have 23 pairs of chromosomes, or 46 in all. Along the length of each chromosome are more than 2,000 alleles, which also come in pairs. Alleles carry specific instructions for each cell.

Walther Flemming (1843—1905)

German scientist Walther Flemming was interested in cell division and chromosomes. In 1882, he published a book that illustrated and described cell division, which he called mitosis.

Human body cells—muscle cells, liver cells, heart cells, and more—reproduce asexually in a process called mitosis. Bacteria cells and plant cells can also reproduce on their own.

Each chromosome has two identical strands called chromatids. The strands are pinched together by a centromere, giving the chromosome its X-like appearance.

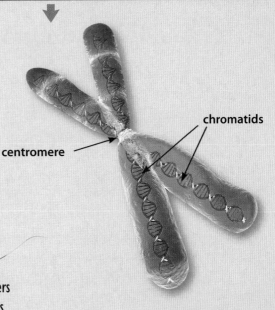

chromatids

centromere

Mitosis

Body cells are constantly dividing and reproducing in a process called mitosis. During mitosis, a cell divides and forms two new cells.

prophase—dense nuclear material condenses into fibers called chromosomes

metaphase—chromosomes line up in the center of the cell; the centromere divides, and the parts move to opposite ends of the cell

anaphase—two chromatids separate and also move to opposite ends

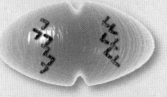

telophase—nuclei form around each chromatid

cytokinesis—cell has become two cells; cell division is complete

Cell during anaphase

Cell Copies

How long do you think it takes one cell to make a copy of itself? It depends on the cell. The time varies with each organism and cell type. A sea urchin cell takes about two hours to duplicate, while a human liver cell takes about 22 hours.

9

Sexual Reproduction

Sex cells, which are different from body cells, are formed in a process called meiosis. The purpose of sex cells is to produce a new individual. Offspring come from the joining of male and female sex cells.

The male sex cell is called a sperm, and the female sex cell is called an egg. Each sex cell only has 23 chromosomes, not 46 chromosomes like body cells have. The sperm contributes 23 chromosomes to the offspring, and so does the egg. Fertilization occurs when the sperm and the egg combine. Half the traits of an offspring come from the mother, and half come from the father.

The new cell, or embryo, has 46 chromosomes. This single cell divides again and again by mitosis. The new cells group and specialize to form a new living being.

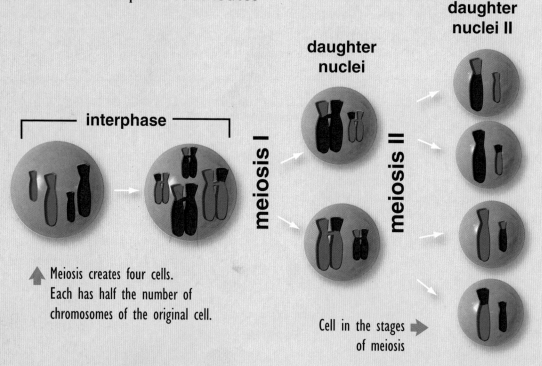

daughter nuclei II

daughter nuclei

interphase

meiosis I

meiosis II

Meiosis creates four cells. Each has half the number of chromosomes of the original cell.

Cell in the stages ➡ of meiosis

Seeing Chromosomes

In 1844, Karl Nägeli found a way to see chromosomes better. He used a special stain that made them easier to see under a microscope. When he looked at a stained cell, he could see the process of cell growth and division. Try staining onion cells or potato cells with iodine. Then look at them under a microscope to see what Nägeli saw.

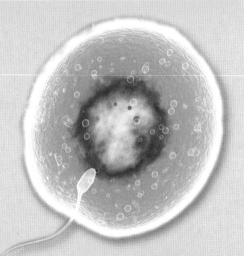

▲ A sperm cell fertilizes an egg cell during sexual reproduction.

Identical Twins

Identical twins are a unique combination of sexual and asexual reproduction. First, a female egg is fertilized sexuall' by a male sperm. Then the fertilized cell divides—in asexu reproduction. Now there are two cells, or two embryos. The embryos develop into two babies—identical twins—with the same genetic makeup.

Potato Chromosomes

Each plant and animal has its own number of chromosomes. Potatoes have 48 chromosomes, while humans have 46. The number doesn't mean how complex an organism is. It's the number of alleles on the chromosomes that determines that.

The XY System

Chromosomes decide if offspring will be female or male. In 1905, scientists discovered that females have two of the same kind of sex chromosomes (XX). Males have two different sex chromosomes (XY). How these chromosomes combine in sexual reproduction determines if the offspring will be a girl or a boy. If the baby is a girl, she inherited two X chromosomes, one from her mother and one from her father. If a boy is born, he got an X chromosome from his mother and a Y chromosome from his father.

A baby's cells work a lot like the parents' cells. Blonde parents usually have blonde children, and entire families can have the same kind of noses or shoulders. In 1902, American geneticist Walter Sutton developed a theory called the chromosome theory of inheritance. It said that parents pass chromosomes to their offspring.

A normal cell contains a full set of chromosomes, or 23 pairs. Each pair is made up of one chromosome from the mother and one from the father. If the father is blonde and the mother is blonde, the chromosomes they give their baby will have blonde alleles, and the baby will have blonde hair.

Walter Sutton
(1877—1916)

Walter Sutton was born in New York but moved to a ranch in Kansas when he was 10. He attended college to become an engineer, but one summer he had to take care of his family members who were very ill with typhoid fever. One of his brothers died. As a result, Sutton decided to study biology in order to become a doctor. Sutton ended up making significant contributions to the science of genetics.

Chromosomes are so small that they can only be seen when they bunch together.

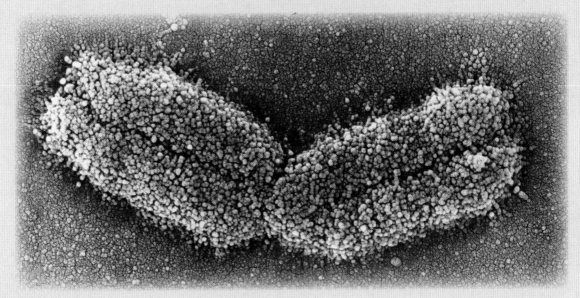

Mixed Alleles

If you get all your chromosomes from your mother and father, then why don't you look just like them? Family members usually resemble one another. But sometimes they look very different from one another. One child may be tall, and another may be short. Your mother and father may have dark hair, but your hair might be light brown or red.

This occurs because each gene carries a variety of alternate forms. These alternate forms are called gene alleles. The gene that determines the color of your hair has many alleles, or variations of the gene. One of the alleles could make your hair black. Another allele might produce brown, red, or blonde hair.

Did You Know?

For many animals, black fur color is dominant and white is recessive. Litters of puppies can be a mixture of black and white puppies. It all depends on which combination of alleles they receive.

You inherit one allele for each gene from your father and one from your mother. Gene alleles get mixed up during reproduction. How those alleles mix produces a unique person.

When a mother and father do not have the same type of alleles, the baby gets a mixture of alleles for its chromosomes. The father may have blonde hair alleles, and the mother's alleles may produce black hair. The baby's cells try to follow both sets of instructions at the same time. What color hair do you think the baby will have? It depends on which alleles are dominant.

Babies inherit alleles for every kind of trait. The way alleles combine determines what a baby looks like. Some alleles are dominant, and others are

Mixing Chromosomes

During the process of meiosis, the chromosomes can get mixed up. They can recombine in a number of new ways. These new combinations give a variety of genetic possibilities for the offspring.

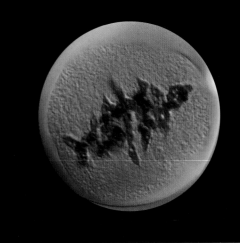

recessive. If two dominant alleles are present, the dominant trait will show up. If a chromosome has two recessive alleles, the recessive trait will show up. But if a dominant allele and a recessive allele are present, the dominant trait will most likely win.

Earlobes are good examples of dominant and recessive alleles. If your mother inherited two recessive alleles for attached earlobes, she got attached earlobes. Let's say your father inherited a dominant allele for unattached earlobes and a recessive allele for attached earlobes. The allele for unattached earlobes is dominant, so your father got unattached earlobes.

But let's not stop there. What kind of earlobes will you have? First, you will get one of your mother's recessive alleles. But the rest depends on whether you inherit your father's dominant or recessive allele. If you get his dominant allele, you will have unattached earlobes. If you get his recessive allele, you will have attached earlobes.

Mother passes		Father passes		Child has
unattached earlobe (D)	+	unattached earlobe (D)	=	unattached earlobe (D)
unnattached earlobe (D)	+	attached earlobe (R)	=	unattached earlobe (D)
attached earlobe (R)	+	attached earlobe (R)	=	attached earlobe (R)

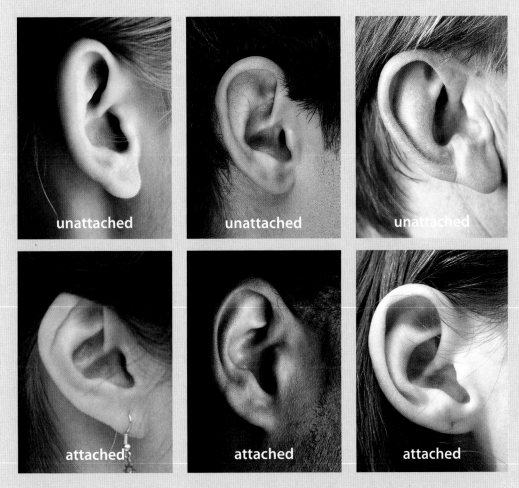

unattached   unattached   unattached

attached   attached   attached

What happens when earlobe alleles combine? The allele for unattached earlobes is dominant (D), and the allele for attached earlobes is recessive (R). In order to get attached earlobes, you must receive the recessive allele from both parents.

Once scientists knew how dominant and recessive alleles worked, they mapped them out. Reginald Punnett, a British geneticist, developed the Punnett Square, a way to diagram allele combinations and show the chance of a specific trait appearing.

The Punnett Square below shows the chance that dark or light hair will appear in a child. The mother has a dark allele (B) and a light allele (b), while the father has two light alleles (bb). But the mother's egg and the father's sperm will have only one allele each. We know that the father's sperm will contain a light allele, but the mother's egg could have either a dark or a light allele.

The Punnett Square shows the various ways their alleles could combine in their offspring.

▲ Reginald Punnett and William Bateson helped establish the new science of genetics in 1900. Bateson was the first to use the word *genetics*. It comes from the Greek word *genno*, which means to give birth.

B = dark-hair allele (dominant)
b = light-hair allele (recessive)

	Father's allele b	Father's allele b
Mother's allele B	Bb	Bb
Mother's allele b	bb	bb

There are two chances out of four (50 percent) that the child will have dark hair. There are also two chances out of four (50 percent) that the child will have light hair. We won't know the hair color until the baby is born.

In something called incomplete dominance, both the dominant and recessive alleles are expressed in the offspring. This creates a blended or combined characteristic.

An example is the color of a flower. One allele for the color red and one for white (no pigment) can combine to make a pink flower.

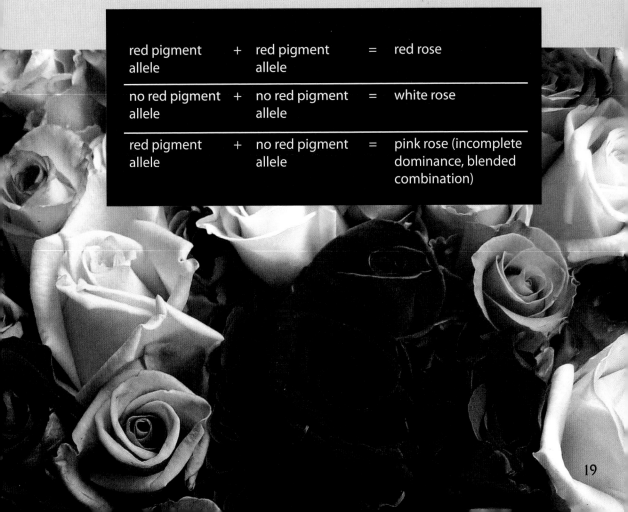

red pigment allele	+	red pigment allele	= red rose
no red pigment allele	+	no red pigment allele	= white rose
red pigment allele	+	no red pigment allele	= pink rose (incomplete dominance, blended combination)

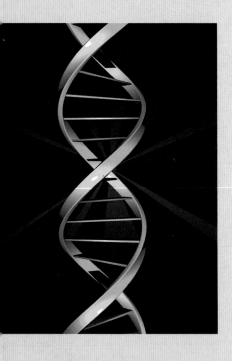

Genes are made up of a chemical called deoxyribonucleic acid—DNA for short. Genes also contain proteins. Scientists in the late 1800s believed that proteins carried genetic information and DNA supported cell reproduction. But in the early 1950s, scientists proved that DNA—not protein—contains the genetic information in alleles.

DNA is the blueprint for cells. Your DNA tells your body how to put certain materials together to produce certain traits. The DNA molecule is very large and is in the shape of a double helix, something like a twisted ladder.

Did You Know?

Each individual has a unique set of fingerprints that form as tiny wrinkles on a baby's fingers. Even identical twins have different fingerprints. Although their DNA is the same, their fingerprints are unique.

Most of the time, DNA is just a big mass that looks like a heap of tangled yarn. But it changes when a cell needs to produce another cell. The DNA untangles into the rodlike forms we recognize as chromosomes. Each chromosome holds a very long DNA molecule.

DNA Fun Fact

If you stretched out all the DNA in your body, it would be long enough to reach from Earth to the moon 6,000 times.

Even the smallest bit of human evidence can contain DNA. Police are careful to preserve crime scenes so every bit of evidence can be found and used to convict criminals. Perhaps no one saw the crime being committed, but DNA will tell the tale.

Double Helix

A double helix is a double-stranded DNA molecule in which two strands of DNA spiral around each other. The two strands have identical copies of all the information needed to make a human being. Having identical copies makes it easier for cells to use DNA. If one strand is being used, the other one can be used.

It's easier to understand how cells use DNA if you look at a zipper. Imagine a double helix coming together and apart like the two sides of a zipper closing and opening. The DNA molecule "unzips" down the middle of its two strands. Then proteins in the cell "read" one or both the strands, and the genes in the strand tell the proteins what to do.

Students learned to build a model of a DNA double helix.

▲ Rosalind Franklin (1920–1958)

In the early 1950s, Rosalind Franklin produced the first clear photograph of DNA. In 1953, James D. Watson and Francis Crick used her ideas as a basis for their publication about DNA's double-helix structure. They used Franklin's research and picture of DNA. In 1962, Watson, Crick, and another scientist Maurice Wilkins received the Nobel Prize in medicine for their work on DNA.

Barbara McClintock (1902—1992)

In 1983, Barbara McClintock won the Nobel Prize in medicine for her work in genetic research. Her career, which began with chromosome research in the 1920s, lasted nearly 70 years. She became one of the foremost scientists in the field of genetics. McClintock died in 1992 at the age of 90.

Human Genome Project

In 1990, two U.S. agencies joined together to accomplish a common goal. They were the U.S. Department of Energy and the National Institutes of Health. Together they coordinated the Human Genome Project, which turned into a 13-year task. Other countries also contributed to the project. The Wellcome Trust of the United Kingdom was a major partner. Japan, France, Germany, China, and other countries were also involved.

Wendy Bickmore

Wendy Bickmore is a genetic researcher from the United Kingdom. She conducts research to discover where human chromosomes and genes are located in cells' nuclei. She also studies how their positions affect them.

The Human Genome Project's goals were:

- Identify all the genes in human DNA (approximately 20,000 to 25,000)

- Determine the sequence of the chemical base pairs that make up human DNA (about 3 billion of them)

- Develop databases to store this information

- Improve tools for gathering data

- Transfer related technologies to the public

- Address the issues that may arise from the project, including ethical, legal, and social issues

Anna Starzinski-Powitz

Anna Starzinski-Powitz is a German research scientist who studied genetics and the functions of cells. She earned her degrees in the 1970s, when Germany didn't support women becoming researchers. Even today, people who don't know she is a woman call her Herr Professor (Herr is the German word for Mister).

Update

In 2000, U.S. President Bill Clinton and U.K. Prime Minister Tony Blair agreed that their countries would work together on the project. They believed the public should have free access to all Human Genome Project data.

In addition, they encouraged private companies to invest in gene-based technology. They also wanted researchers to be able to use this information. The two leaders hoped the research would lead to the development of new medicines. There was a challenge to learn 90 percent of the sequences of DNA within five years.

Craig Venter, the CEO of a company called Celera Genomics, worked on the project privately. He was competing with Francis S. Collins and the Human Genome Project. Finally, on April 14, 2003, a joint press release announced that both groups had completed the project. They had sequenced 99 percent of the genome with 99.99 percent accuracy. They beat the challenge by two years.

Mutations

Sometimes perfectly normal cells mutate when something causes their genetic information to change. Copying errors during cell division can produce a mutated cell. Mutations are also caused by exposure to radiation, chemicals, or viruses.

Sometimes mutations are beneficial, and other times they have no effect at all. But many times they are harmful. Some mutations result in offspring having birth defects or genetic disorders. Some children end up with too many chromosomes, and others have too few.

Harmful Mutations

Individuals with Down syndrome have an extra chromosome—three instead of two in Pair 21. This extra chromosome causes people with Down syndrome to have a distinct physical appearance and some degree of mental retardation.

Did You Know?

One in 10 cats in New England has six or seven toes on each paw. Most likely, this trait has been inherited from a cat with extra toes that arrived in the 1600s with the Pilgrims.

Gene mutation also causes a disease called cystic fibrosis. The gene that mutates is called CFTR (cystic fibrosis transmembrane conductance regulator). There is no cure for this disease, which mainly affects a person's lungs and digestive system. Most people with the disease die in their 20s or 30s.

Mutations Can Block Disease

Some mutated genes are beneficial. In the 1300s, a genetic mutation helped people become immune to the bubonic plague. But we didn't know this until much later, in the 20th century when Dr. Stephen J. O'Brien studied descendants of people who had survived the plague. He concluded that the mutated CCR5 gene, delta 32, may have prevented the plague from entering a person's white blood cells.

Recent work with HIV, the virus that causes AIDS, shows that it affects the immune system in a similar way. Drug companies are trying to develop a drug that will copy delta 32. They hope it will block HIV.

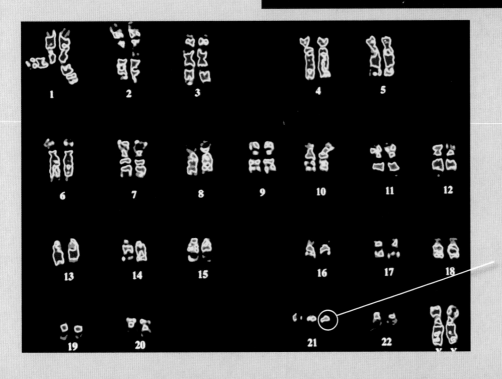

People with Down syndrome have an extra chromosome in Pair 21.

27

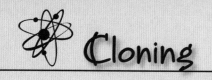
Clones have often made interesting characters in science fiction movies. But cloning is no longer just for science fiction. Now there is real news about cloned animals and cloned body parts. There's even talk about secretly cloned human beings.

But what is a clone? A clone is the identical copy of another organism. Both organisms have the exact same genes. Natural clones are all around us—plant clones are everywhere, and bacteria and other one-celled organisms make clones whenever they reproduce. The cell makes an exact copy of itself and then divides into two identical cells. There are even natural human clones—identical twins.

But scientists can now make clones in laboratories. In 1996, they cloned the first animal—a female sheep named Dolly. Those responsible for Dolly were scientists Ian Wilmut and Keith Campbell, along with other scientists at the Roslin Institute in Scotland. Dolly died on February 14, 2003. After Dolly, goats, pigs, mice, and cows were also cloned.

Did You Know?

The first cloned living thing was a tadpole that was cloned in 1962.

Could Human Clones Be Next?

No one knows for sure if scientists will be able to clone a whole human being. But many people believe it would be wrong to clone humans. Some believe cloning might be used to make a perfect race or get rid of undesirable human traits. Others believe cloning would reduce variety in the human gene pool, which would be a dangerous thing to do. Variety helps create stronger, healthier people. There are still many questions about human cloning that scientists have not been able to answer.

Some scientists believe cloning would be beneficial. They believe cloning would help cure diseases such as Parkinson's disease and Alzheimer's. But most think we should learn more about cloning before we use the process with people. What do you think?

Dolly, a cloned sheep, and her firstborn lamb, Bonnie

The Trouble With Cloning

It took scientists 227 tries to get Dolly, a cloned sheep. Early clones were seriously deformed and died soon after they were born. The scientists who cloned Dolly don't think humans should be cloned because the risks are too high.

In this lab, you will survey your family members and friends to find out how many of them display certain dominant or recessive traits. Look for the following trait pairs:

Dominant	Recessive
unattached earlobes	attached earlobes
can roll tongue in a *U* shape	can't roll tongue in a *U* shape
no widow's peak	widow's peak
brown eyes	gray, green, or blue eyes
index finger shorter than ring finger	ring finger shorter than index finger
dark hair	light hair
non-red hair	red hair
curly hair	straight hair

Materials

- paper
- pencil
- computer with spreadsheet application and a printer (optional)

Procedure

1 On a sheet of paper, list all the dominant and recessive characteristics found on the Dominant/Recessive chart shown above. Put a box to the left of each characteristic. At the top of the page, put a line for the name of the person you will be interviewing.

2 Make at least 10 copies of your list.

3 Interview 10 or more family members and friends. Use a separate sheet for each interview. Ask them which characteristics they have and put checkmarks in the boxes next to those characteristics.

4 When you are finished with all your interviews, make a chart with two columns. Label the left column "Characteristics" and list all characteristics. Label the right column "Number."

5 Add up the number of boxes you checked for each characteristic. Put the total number next to the characteristic on your chart.

6 Create a bar graph to display your results. You can use a computer and a printer to do this, if one is available.

7 Summarize your results.

Conclusion

Dominant traits show up more often than recessive traits. Genetic traits show up in predictable patterns within families. Did you reach the same conclusion?

Idea for Further Study

Use genetics as a keyword to research genetic traits on the Internet. Make a poster to share the most interesting information you find.

William Bateson (1861–1926)
British geneticist who helped establish the science of genetics in 1900; first scientist to use the word *genetics*

Walther Flemming (1843–1905)
Investigated cell division and how chromosomes distribute to the second nucleus; called process mitosis

Rosalind Franklin (1920–1958)
English scientist who made significant contributions to understanding the structure of DNA

Barbara McClintock (1902–1992)
Won the Nobel Prize in medicine in 1983 for her work on genetic research

Gregor Mendel (1822–1884)
Priest and scientist who came to be called the father of modern genetics; studied how pea plants inherit specific traits and follow certain laws, which came to be called the Mendellian laws of inheritance

Karl Nägeli (1817–1891)
Swiss botanist who studied plant cells and used a special
stain to see chromosomes better under a microscope;
credited with observing cell growth and division

Reginald Punnett (1875–1967)
British geneticist who helped establish the science of
genetics in 1900; best known for his Punnett square, a
tool used to predict the probability of a particular trait
appearing in offspring

Walter Sutton (1877–1916)
American scientist who developed the chromosome
theory of inheritance, which stated that both parents
pass chromosomes to their offspring

James D. Watson (1928–   ), **Francis Crick** (1916–
2004), and **Maurice Wilkins** (1916–2004)
Jointly awarded the 1962 Nobel Prize in medicine for
their discovery of the double-helix structure of DNA

Glossary

AIDS—acquired immune deficiency syndrome; disease of the immune system caused by HIV

alleles—alternate forms of a gene that control a particular characteristic

anaphase—last stage of cell division, during which chromosomes move to opposite ends of the nucleus

asexual reproduction—type of reproduction that does not involve a partner

bubonic plague—contagious disease carried by fleas

cell cycle—process of cell growth, division, and reproduction

centromere—center of a human chromosome where two chromatids join

chromatid—one of the two strands of a chromosome that is visible during the process of cell division

chromosome—threadlike structure in the nucleus of a cell that carries genes

clone—identical copy of another organism

cytokinesis—division of the cytoplasm during the cell cycle

DNA—deoxyribonucleic acid; the chemical of which genes are made

dominant allele—gene most likely to produce a particular trait in offspring

double helix—spiral structure of DNA

gene—basic unit of heredity

generation—all the offspring from one stage of descent from a common ancestor

genetics—branch of biology that involves studying heredity and genetic variations

Human Genome Project—international research program that recorded the entire human genetic code

HIV—human immunodeficiency virus that causes AIDS

incomplete dominance—both the dominant and recessive gene alleles show, creating a blended or combined characteristic

interphase—phase in the cell cycle in which the cell is resting or growing but not dividing

meiosis—cell division that produces eggs and sperm, which have half the usual number of chromosomes

metaphase—second phase of cell division in which the chromosomes line up in order to separate

mitosis—cell division that creates two cells with the same number of chromosomes as the parent cell

mutation—a change resulting in a new trait

prophase—first phase in cell division in which chromosomes condense and are seen as two chromatids

reproduction—production of young plants and animals through either a sexual or an asexual process

recessive allele—gene most likely to stay "hidden"

sexual reproduction—reproduction involving a male and a female, with each contributing half of the genetic makeup of the offspring

telophase—phase of cell division in which a nucleus forms around each chromatid

trait—genetically determined condition or characteristic

1340s	Bubonic plague strikes Europe, killing millions of people
1844	Karl Nägeli sees the process of cell growth and division under a microscope
1856	Gregor Mendel begins studying pea plants; discovers that plants pass along dominant and recessive traits
1882	Walther Flemming publishes a book that illustrates and describes cell division
1900	Reginald Punnett and William Bateson establish the new science of genetics at Cambridge University
1902	Walter Sutton determines that chromosomes may be the carriers of inherited characteristics; develops the chromosome theory of inheritance
1905	Female mammals are found to have two X chromosomes; male mammals are found to have an XY pair
1926	Hermann J. Muller finds that X-rays can cause genetic mutations
1953	DNA structure is discovered by James Watson and Francis Crick; their work is based on the work of Rosalind Franklin
1954	Scientists discover that humans have 46 chromosomes

1962	Scientists clone a tadpole
1969	First single gene is isolated
1982	Pharmaceutical company makes the first genetically engineered medicine: human insulin made from a bacterium
1983	First artificial chromosome is developed
1983	Barbara McClintock wins the Nobel Prize in medicine for her work in genetics
1984	Allan Wilson and Russell Higuchi are the first to clone genes from an extinct species
1988	First genetically engineered mouse is developed
1994	Genetically engineered tomatoes that ripen more slowly are introduced into the marketplace
1996	Female sheep named Dolly is the first animal cloned; she dies in 2003
2003	The Human Genome Project is completed; 99 percent of DNA is sequenced
2008	Researchers study the genetics of maize in order to find ways to improve the crop's level of vitamin A; this would improve the health of people in Africa and Latin America, where maize is a large part of their diet

Day, Trevor. *Genetics*. San Diego: Blackbirch Press, 2004.

George, Linda. *Gene Therapy*. San Diego: Blackbirch Press, 2003.

Glimm, Adele. *Gene Hunter: The Story of Neuropsychologist Nancy Wexler*. New York: Franklin Watts, 2005.

Stille, Darlene. *Genetics: A Living Blueprint*. Minneapolis: Compass Point Books, 2006.

Walker, Richard. *Genes and DNA*. Boston: Kingfisher, 2003.

On the Web

For more information on this topic, use FactHound.

1. Go to *www.facthound.com*

2. Type in this book ID: 0756539560

3. Click on the *Fetch It* button.

FactHound will find the best Web sites for you.

Index

About the Author

Lynn Van Gorp

Lynn Van Gorp graduated with a master of science degree from the University of Calgary, Canada, and did additional graduate work at the University of Washington, Seattle, and the University of California, Irvine. She has taught for more than 30 years, at the elementary and middle-school levels and at the university level. Her educational focus areas include science, reading, and technology. She has written a number of student- and teacher-based curriculum-related publications.

Image Credits